CONTENTS

• INTRODUCTION •

The space shuttle reaches the final minutes of countdown. Suddenly there's a beep heard at mission control. A red light flashes. Something is wrong. Air pressure is destabilized in sector 4 (or something like that). Liftoff is delayed until the problem is righted.

You're finishing your paper for school on the word processor. All at once you notice the screen is showing *B*'s when you're typing *A*'s, and the return key doesn't work. Time to fix the computer.

Relationships can be like this, too. For example, maybe you remember some good times with your parents last year or the year before. But then something went wrong. Or maybe you don't hang out with your "best friend" anymore because it seems like there's a wall between you. There's tremendous potential in these relationships, if only you can fix the glitch.

The glitches that occur in relationships are sometimes called "dysfunctions." Lately there's been a lot of talk about "dysfunctional families." You've seen the effects—if not in your own family, in other homes around you. Dysfunctional families struggle with problems like unhealthy competition, lack of communication, even addictions and violence.

Dysfunctions can also happen in the "family of God," the body of Christ. A church or Christian youth group should be a place of caring fellowship, lively worship, radiant outreach. But sometimes the red lights flash and the beeps warn us that something is wrong. We need to fix those things.

This Spiritual Adventure is about pinpointing some of those dysfunctions and letting Christ put our relationships back together (or keep them healthy). Christ has tons of power that he wants to use in your life. We'll find that there are some simple habits such as good communication, acceptance, playfulness and prayer that will work wonders in our relationships. The next few pages tell how you can start developing those habits during this Adventure, as you grow closer to others and closer to Christ.

● ● ●

HOW TO USE THIS JOURNAL

Read pages 4-14 before the Adventure starts. That will give you an overview of what you'll be doing during the 50 days of the Adventure. Don't be overwhelmed by the five "action steps." Once the Adventure starts, all you'll need to do is . . .

Follow the day-by-day instructions. They begin on page 15. Notice that there is a Scripture passage to read each day, and questions to answer (this is all part of Action Step 1). We'll also give you reminders to help you keep up with the other action steps.

Take a little time to think about each day's Scripture and pray. We figure this will take about 10 minutes a day, with a little extra time for some of the other steps.

But don't go crazy! If you miss a day, don't try to make it up. Just find the current day in the journal and start there.

Make it yours. This journal is for *your* spiritual growth, right? We're not trying to fit you into some box of our making. The Scripture questions and the prayer (Action Step 3) are designed to get you interacting with God. Trust his Spirit to lead you along this Adventure.

Try to do all five action steps. They're created to fit together. But if you don't have time for all that, skip one. Take the steps you need to take to help you grow closer to God and others.

Have fun with this Adventure. If you get harried because you don't know how to affirm people and your prayer partner can't meet on your free day and you have no idea what to do for Action Step 4, you're missing the point. Relax. Breathe. Smile. Laugh. Enjoy each step of this journey.

● ● ●

WHERE TO START

Take a few minutes *now* to read about the action steps (pages 4-14). Then just wait for the Adventure to begin. For a head start, do the Friday and Saturday warm-up days before Day 1 of the Adventure. They're on pages 15-16.

● ● ●

PAY ATTENTION!

Your mind is sailing through the sky with the birds or running barefoot in the grass, daydreaming about your hot date. Suddenly you hear your name in the distance. You know that voice, it sounds like . . . your teacher.

"Would you complete problem 13 and calculate the length of the hypotenuse?"

"I'm sorry," you say. "I wasn't listening."

You know that story. If not in class, maybe with your parents or a friend. You tune out. Hey, they say it's an MTV generation. Give me a new picture every 10 seconds or I lose interest.

I know it's happened to you in church. Even the most interesting pastors preach through Leviticus every so often, and your mind changes channels. Don't worry; it happens to everyone.

So here's our first "dysfunction," the first glitch in our relationships: lack of listening. People in unhealthy churches or youth groups, just like those in unhealthy homes, don't listen to each other. Even worse, they can stop listening to God. And then it's vicious-cycle time, because how are you going to fix your glitches if you don't pay attention to the One who can help you?

Our first action step, then, is pretty simple: Read your Bible every day. But don't just read it—listen to God speak through his Word. You'll be amazed at what you discover about growing closer to Christ and other believers.

•• ▶ JUST DO IT!

Read the Scripture passage assigned for each day in this journal, and answer the questions that follow. Note that Saturday and Sunday are usually treated as one day. Each week the Scripture readings deal with a specific area where we can grow in our relationships. The "strategy session" before each Friday in the journal tells about the topics for the coming week.

Remember, if you miss a day or two, don't try to make them up. Just start fresh with the current day in the journal.

● ● ●

ACTION STEP 2 · AFFIRM OTHERS

"**W**inning isn't everything. It's the only thing."

That may sound cool in the locker room, but it's no way to live your life. And yet some families operate that way. If you're a star athlete, straight-*A* student, high achiever, you get hugs and praises from your folks. But when you drop the pass or get *C's* in a tough course—well, then you almost think your parents hardly know you exist. It's as if you have to earn their love with satisfactory performance.

Sadly, this sort of thing happens in churches and youth groups, too. Every group has its "stars," the ones who lead, teach, answer all the questions, plan the socials and serve on all the committees. Don't get me wrong; these are usually wonderful people. But there are a lot of other wonderful people around, too—and they're often forgotten.

Just because you don't take all the pictures on the youth group retreats, that doesn't mean you don't have talents God can use. And just because you sometimes get lost trying to look up Zephaniah in your Bible, that doesn't mean you're not a good Christian.

You see, Jesus doesn't operate on a "star system." He loves all of us—the people up front and the people in the pews. He doesn't insist that we strive to earn his affection. He just wants us to love him in any way we can.

There are lots of "unsung heroes" in every church. The janitor, the person who types the bulletin, those who tend the nursery, the kid who sets up the chairs for Sunday school. These people and others perform tasks that may not be noticed very much. But they deserve affirmation. You can be the one who reminds them of how much Jesus must appreciate them.

• • ▶ JUST DO IT!

Once each week, choose someone (maybe in your church or

youth group) to affirm, someone you think Jesus would like to say some encouraging things to. Don't go for the "stars." Look for the unsung heroes, those who display inner attitudes of love, humility and service.

Say your affirming words in person, or with a note or phone call. Here are some things you might say:

> "I think it's really great that you _____
> [fill in the "unsung" stuff the person does]."
>
> "Your _____ [some trait like calmness or a sense of humor] is really cool. I appreciate that."
>
> "Your love for Jesus really came through when you _____ [fill in a specific thing the person did]."

To keep track of your progress, make a note on page 63 of the affirming words you say each week.

ACTION STEP 3

STOP THE BLAME-SHAME SYNDROME

Some families seem to have a designated scapegoat. "If Andy weren't so . . . , we'd be fine."

In those cases, two things happen. **1.** Andy feels like scum. That's shame. **2.** The rest of the family never looks at their own problems—it's all Andy's fault. That's blame.

What about your church? Do you have a favorite scapegoat? Do you tend to blame everything (possibly even your own lack of spiritual growth) on the pastor, youth leader, Sunday school teacher or a kid in your group?

Often, young people blame the older people for making the church too traditional or dull. If that's your situation, you may find things will improve if you stop looking for someone to blame and get more involved yourself.

But the blame-shame syndrome can poison a youth group, too. "Jenny always brings her guitar, but she only knows three chords." "Justin always makes fun of everyone." "Diana always wants things her own way." Suddenly a youth group is not about pleasing God or learning the Bible or enjoying each other—it's all about who's right and who's wrong.

So how do you stop the blame-shame syndrome? It starts in your own heart. And the best way to change your heart is through prayer.

•• ▶ JUST DO IT!

At least once a day, pray the following prayer. Make it your own. Feel free to change the words a little to make it fit your situation. And if "blame-shame" isn't a problem for you, great! Keep it that way by using this prayer as a reminder.

A PRAYER FOR
THE BODY OF CHRIST

Father,
I know that no church (or youth group) is perfect,
so help me not to be surprised
when problems arise.
Keep me from pointing a finger of blame at others;
guard my tongue from shameful remarks.
Give me the courage to do my part
to make our church a better place.
And thank you for graciously allowing me
to be a member of your wonderful family.
Amen.

BEAT UNHEALTHY COMPETITION

C **ompetition** can be fun and healthy. But when you overdo it, it can lead to uncaring attitudes, pride, bitterness or insecurity.

You probably know families where the brothers and sisters are always fighting for the upper hand. You may know church groups where that happens, too.

Why didn't they put *me* on the leadership committee? Why do they always ask *him* to pray in youth group? I wish our sponsors would pay more attention to *me* instead of always talking to *her.* Sound familiar?

The Bible, however, gives a different picture of the church—*not a battlefield but a body.* We shouldn't be out to be better Christians than everyone else, but to help everyone grow in Christ together. We don't have to fight to gain the upper hand; instead we should give one another helping hands and pick each other up.

Bodies have different parts that specialize in different things. Imagine the chaos if every part insisted on being an eye or a hand or a mouth. Just as our physical bodies need different parts doing dif-ferent things, so the body of Christ needs different people in different roles.

You have special abilities to offer your church. This action step will give you a chance to try a job in your church you've never done before. Hopefully it will be fun, and you might just discover a hidden talent. Or, you may gain a new appreciation for the people who regu-larly do that task.

Have fun with this action step. Remember, it will be a learning experience for everyone.

▶ JUST DO IT!

1. When you're ready to start this action step, go through the list below, marking any jobs you've never done in your church.

2. Go back over the ones you've checked and circle the one you'd most like to try.

3. Talk to the person in charge of that ministry to see if there's a way you could get involved. Explain that you're not making a long-term commitment; you just want to try the task once. Be ready with a second or third choice in case the job you chose first isn't available.

4. After completing the task, fill out the brief evaluation form on page 64.

● ● ●

The List

- ❏ Work in the nursery
- ❏ Serve coffee in the fellowship time
- ❏ Clean up after a special event
- ❏ Set up for Communion
- ❏ Help prepare the bulletin
- ❏ Cook for a church supper
- ❏ Deliver food or clothes to a needy family
- ❏ Volunteer to help with repair work in the church building
- ❏ Greet newcomers
- ❏ Visit a shut-in
- ❏ Write to a missionary (or a missionary's kids)
- ❏ Sign up for the prayer chain (your church secretary could probably tell you how)
- ❏ Read the Scripture in a worship service
- ❏ Make a flower arrangement for the sanctuary
- ❏ Work in the audio-visual booth
- ❏ Plan a social event for the youth group
- ❏ Usher
- ❏ Sing in the choir
- ❏ Write an article for the church newsletter
- ❏ Help plan the worship service
- ❏ Teach a children's Sunday school class
- ❏ Lead a youth group Bible study
- ❏ Play a musical instrument in the worship service
- ❏ Give a children's sermon
- ❏ Come up with your own idea of something you could do for your church _____

ACTION STEP 5

OPEN UP TO A PRAYER PARTNER

Bart Simpson has gotten some bad press. Sure, he's rude and mischief-minded. But there's one thing I like about him—he smashes denial. Mom and Dad can be playing their games, pretending everything's okay. And then Bart comes along, saying, "Yo! Something's wrong here! Wake up and smell the bananas!"

Denial is another of those glitches we find in families and churches. We've become masters of the "cover-up." If we admit there's a problem, we have to fix it. It's easier to ignore it.

This happens often in our spiritual lives. We think we're all supposed to be "good Christians." We never have any doubts, any sins, any weaknesses, right? WRONG! We need to be honest with one another. Then we can help each other and grow in our relationship with Christ.

We're not suggesting that you get up in front of your church or youth group and say, "Don't have a cow, man! Let's all confess our sins out loud in graphic detail!" But we *are* asking you to team up with one or two other believers in a special "prayer partnership." This could be the first step toward greater openness and honesty—important ingredients of good relationships.

▶ JUST DO IT!

1. Find one other Christian (maybe two) you can join with in a "prayer partnership." How? Here are some ideas:

- Think about asking one of your friends, such as someone from youth group or a Christian you know at school. It might be easier to open up to a friend than to someone you don't know as well.
- Don't overlook the possibility of teaming with a family member.
- The main thing to look for is trustworthiness. Do you trust this person enough to share honestly with him or her?
- Beware of opposite-sex partnerships. Don't try to use this as a way of developing a romance. Those passions can get in

the way of honest interaction.

● If you can't find a prayer partner on your own, ask your youth leader or pastor to suggest someone.

2. Plan to meet with this person at least four times during the Adventure to talk and pray. Find a time that's good for both of you when you can get together for a little while. If you can't meet in person, you could talk and pray over the phone.

3. Follow the guidelines for each session on pages 32-33. There are a few short questions to get you talking. Some of them are fun, and some are a little more serious. Then there are suggestions for prayer. Try to make the most of your prayer partnership. Don't just gab the time away.

The first session includes signing a simple covenant, or agreement, in which you promise to keep any secrets that are shared.

This action step could be a great way to strengthen a friendship. And remember, when two or three of you gather in Christ's name, he's there with you.

If you need some extra motivation to start a prayer partnership, The Chapel of the Air has put together a short book called Two Are Better than One: A Guide to Prayer Partnerships That Work. *If your church doesn't have copies, ask about it at a Christian bookstore or call the Chapel at 708-668-7292 (in Canada: 416-659-1800).*

HOW NOT TO BE A PRAYER PARTNER

NO, RAMON, WHEN I SAID, 'LET'S CLOSE OUR EYES AND SHARE OUR NEEDS,' THAT'S NOT WHAT I HAD IN MIND.

ACTION STEP Summary

Refer to this list to see how often the various action steps are to be done. (For a full description of the steps, see pp. 4-13.)

▶ DAILY

ACTION STEP 1: Read the Scripture passage for each day in the journal, and answer the questions that follow.

ACTION STEP 3: Pray the Prayer for the Body of Christ, using the words on page 9 as a guide.

▶ WEEKLY

ACTION STEP 2: Choose an "unsung hero" in your church or youth group to affirm with some encouraging words.

▶ FOUR TIMES DURING THE ADVENTURE

ACTION STEP 5: Find a prayer partner and get together at least four times during the Adventure. Use the guidelines on pages 32-33.

▶ ONCE DURING THE ADVENTURE

ACTION STEP 4: Pick a task in your church you've never done before, and make arrangements to try it (just once). Then fill out the form on page 64 to evaluate your experience.

EXTRA RESOURCES: *If your church is doing the Adventure, your pastor may be preaching on the same themes you'll be exploring each week in this journal. You can also hear about these topics on the daily Chapel of the Air radio broadcast. To find out when the program is aired in your area, write and ask for a free radio log. The address is: The Chapel of the Air, Box 30, Wheaton, IL 60189. (in Canada: Box 2000, Waterdown, Ontario L0R 2H0)*

Another resource is a book created specially for this Adventure, called Healing the Dysfunctional Church Family. *Each chapter expands on one of the weekly Adventure topics. If your church doesn't have copies of this book, ask about it at a Christian bookstore. Or, call the Chapel office at 708-668-7292. (In Canada, phone 416-659-1800.)*

TOPIC 1

STRATEGY SESSION

FOCUS: Christians should love each other unconditionally.

CONTRASTING DYSFUNCTION (glitch in relationships): Having to earn approval.

POSSIBLE RESOURCES: Your pastor's sermon; The Chapel of the Air broadcasts; introduction and chapter 1 of *Healing the Dysfunctional Church Family*. (For information on these resources, see p. 14.)

▶ SUGGESTED PRAYER OF PREPARATION

Lord,

I praise you for your unconditional love. You take great pleasure, great joy, great delight in your children. We don't have to earn your love. Because Christ died in our place, we are now acceptable to you. Thank you for your deep compassion for us.

Amen.

FRIDAY

WARM-UP

▼ **READ**
Ephesians 1:3-8

Right away, God is described as one who "blesses" us with "every spiritual blessing." What specific blessings are listed in these verses?

_____

_____

Continued

Which of these blessings means the most to you, and why?

_____

_____

What have we done to deserve these blessings?

_____

    (The answer is NOTHING. We can't earn God's love; he just gives it.)

❏ I've started praying the Prayer for the Body of Christ (see p. 9).

SATURDAY

WARM-UP

▼ READ
Isaiah 49:13-15

In these verses, joy turns to concern and then back to assurance. A key word is compassion. That's the deep-felt love God has for us.

    When was the last time you felt like verse 13? Why did you feel that way?

_____

_____

When was the last time you felt like verse 14? Why?

_____

_____

How does verse 15 make you feel?

_____

_____

❏ I've read over the Topic 1 Strategy Session on p. 15.

In 5:1, we're called "dearly loved children." Loved by whom? By God, of course. How should we respond to that?

_____

_____

That key word, compassion (or compassionate), pops up again in 4:32. The same deep love God has for us is what we should show to others. Is there one person you could be "kind and compassionate" to today or tomorrow? Who and how?

_____

_____

One way to show love to others is in the very down-to-earth suggestion of 4:29. How would you define "unwholesome talk"?

_____

_____

❑ I've read pp. 1-14 to get an idea of what will be happening during this Adventure.

M⊙NDAY

DAY 2

In this chapter, qualities of true love are spelled out. Some are positive ("love is . . .") and some are negative ("love does not . . ."). Choose one positive description that especially grabs you.

_____

Can you come up with an example of this quality from your family or church or youth group?

I saw love in action when_____

_____

_____

Is there a negative description of love that grabs you?

_____

Can you come up with another example—positive or negative?

I saw [did not see] love in action when_____

_____

_____

Which quality do you think is hardest for the people in your church or youth group to live up to?_____

❑ I've started praying the Prayer for the Body of Christ (see p. 9).

TUESDAY

Living "in harmony" means:

- Ⓐ Singing a lot
- Ⓑ Being exactly the same as everyone else
- Ⓒ Accepting the differences of others and getting along with them

Loving others "as brothers" means:

- Ⓐ Fighting a lot
- Ⓑ Acting like the Brady Bunch
- Ⓒ Having a basic loyalty, understanding and appreciation for one another

"Do not repay . . . insult with insult." This is:

- Ⓐ Impossible
- Ⓑ A good idea in general, but it doesn't apply when you're just joking around with the guys you hang around with
- Ⓒ Hard to do, but possible because God gives us compassion.

❏ I'm praying about finding a prayer partner (see pp. 12-13).

"**P**erfect love drives out fear." Think about that. Don't write anything down today. Just think.

Do you have any relationships that are based on fear? With teachers or even certain friends? What about your mom or dad? Are you ever afraid you'll lose their love if you don't "measure up" in some way?

Growing up is a matter of turning fear into love. That's what "perfect" means in that verse—"grown up."

When we were kids, we learned to fear the consequences of disobeying our parents. But somehow, if our relationships are healthy, that fear has to turn to love. Is that happening in your life?

Now, here's something else to chew on: The same thing happens in our relationship with God. "The fear of the Lord is the beginning of knowledge" (Proverbs 1:7), but that's just the beginning. As God showers his unconditional love on us, our fear grows into love. "We love because he first loved us." We do good things not because we're afraid of being punished, but because we want to please God!

Is that where you are?

❏   I'm praying about a new job I could try in my church (see Action Step 4 on pp. 10-11).

Have you found a prayer partner yet? If not, better start looking. Why do you need a prayer partner, anyway? Ecclesiastes 4:9-12 gives you some reasons.

Why are two or three better than one?

_____

_____

Can you give a modern example of this truth? Perhaps from your own experience?

_____

_____

❑ This week I chose someone to affirm, and I've noted what I said on p. 63.

TO[DAYS 6–12]IC 2

FOCUS: Christians should take responsibility to help make their church or youth group better.

CONTRASTING DYSFUNCTION (glitch in relationships): The "blame-shame syndrome"—always pointing a finger of blame at someone else.

POSSIBLE RESOURCES: Your pastor's sermon; The Chapel of the Air broadcasts; chapter 2 of *Healing the Dysfunctional Church Family.* (For information on these resources, see p. 14.)

► SUGGESTED PRAYER OF PREPARATION

> *Lord,*
> *I praise you for the tenderness of your mercy. You don't point a harsh finger of blame at us, or shame us when we sin. But you surprise us with your kindness—and gently call us to a better life.*
> *Amen.*

FR[DAY 6]DAY

▼
READ
Psalm 25:1-7

What does the psalmist want God to do?

_____

How does the psalmist describe God?

_____

_____

Here's some good news. God does forgive, through Christ. Is there a particular sin you want God to clean up? Ask him, and he will.

❏ I'm praying about finding a prayer partner (see pp. 12-13).

This is my favorite chapter in the whole Bible, so read it twice if you can. Here are some of the things I like:

Verse 1—"all my inmost being." We praise God with all of who we are, inside and out.

Verse 9—"he will not always accuse." The blame-shame syndrome gets turned on its ear. If anyone could put us to shame, it's God—he's perfect. He could make us feel really rotten for being so sinful, but he doesn't. He points out our sin, and then he forgives us.

Verse 12—How far is the east from the west? Real far.

Verse 13—"compassion." How many times have we seen that word so far? Here the word implies a sense of understanding. A little kid can say something really stupid or embarrassing, and no one holds it against him because he's just a kid. That's the idea here.

What's *your* favorite part of this psalm?

❏ I'm praying the Prayer for the Body of Christ.

M○NDAY

DAY 9

READ
John 8:1-11

Why did the teachers and Pharisees bring up this matter?

_____

_____

How would you have felt if you had been in the woman's place?

_____

_____

_____

_____

Why do you think Jesus didn't throw stones? (He could have, because he was "without sin.")

_____

_____

_____

_____

Do you know someone who feels accused and needs to be forgiven and picked up? How can you help?

_____

_____

_____

❑ I've found a prayer partner, and we've decided when we'll get together for the first time. (See pp. 12-13.)

TUESDAY

DAY 10

READ
Matthew 7:1-5

When was the last time someone judged you? Do you think this person had a right to judge you? How did you respond?

_____

_____

In your opinion, who is most to blame for the problems of your church or youth group? Don't write this down, but just think of a person. Now, what do you think is this person's problem? He/she is too_____

What happens if you judge yourself by the same standard? Do you ever act the same way? How does this change your outlook?

_____

_____

❏ I've chosen a job to try in my church. This week I'll talk to the person in charge of that ministry. (See Action Step 4 on pp. 10-11.)

NOTES FOR A THREE-ACT PLAY

ACT I: The Grumbling
What was the people's complaint?

_____

ACT II: The Case for Taking Canaan
Who would you cast in the roles of Joshua and Caleb? Why?

_____

_____

How do you think these guys felt?_____

ACT III: God Speaks
In modern terms, what was his message?

_____

Looking back at the story, who was blaming whom?

_____

Who do you think was really to blame? _____

Would the people have been better off if they hadn't been so quick to blame someone else? How?

_____

❏   I'm praying the Prayer for the Body of Christ.

THURSDAY

READ
Matthew 18:19, 20

D **O** you have a prayer partner yet? Remember, if you're going to get together four times during the Adventure, you'll need to get started soon.

Now, let's suppose someone says, "Our team was in the state finals, and I got together with a couple of friends from school and we prayed that we'd win. But we got clobbered instead. Doesn't Matthew 18:19 promise that God will give us whatever we pray for?" How would you answer?

_____

_____

_____

_____

_____

It's a tough question. If you're bothered by this, you might want to talk with a parent, pastor or youth worker about it. But here are just a few thoughts to chew on.

1. Christ's promise is far greater than a sports victory. He offers his presence, and we're worried about slam dunks!

2. Christ works through our relationships. As we pray together and work together, we have great power. This may help a team play better, but it will also help a church worship and witness better.

3. Other verses say that God gives whatever we ask "in Christ's name." The idea is that we must be seeking Christ's glory, not our own.

❑   This week I chose someone to affirm, and I've noted what I said on p. 63.

TOPIC 3

STRATEGY SESSION

FOCUS: Christians should value the unique abilities of others.

CONTRASTING DYSFUNCTION (glitch in relationships): Unhealthy comparisons and competition.

POSSIBLE RESOURCES: Your pastor's sermon; The Chapel of the Air broadcasts; chapter 3 of *Healing the Dysfunctional Church Family* (see p. 14).

▶ SUGGESTED PRAYER OF PREPARATION

Lord,
I praise you for your marvelous originality in creating your children. You delight in our uniqueness. We don't have to compete with one another, because you have given each of us a special blend of abilities to make your plans happen through us.   *Amen.*

FRIDAY

DAY 13

▼
READ
Psalm 139:13-16

If God did such a good job of creating, what does that say about us? _____

A few years ago, there was a phrase: "God don't make no junk." Do you think today's Scripture supports that? Why or why not?

_____

F.A.W.M. That's what you are. That's what everyone else is, too. Here's a thought: This weekend, every so often, congratulate someone else for being F.A.W.M. You don't even have to say right away what it means—"Fearfully And Wonderfully Made."
How might this change your attitude about others?

_____

Imagine: A. The pastor asks you to preach in his place on Sunday. **B.** Your local major league baseball team wants you to pitch this Friday. **C.** The President or Prime Minister wants to send you on a peace mission to the Middle East.

Gulp. Scary, huh? That's sort of how Moses felt. Have you ever felt like Moses did? When?

_____

The fact is that God had prepared Moses to lead his people. Moses was not recognizing the abilities God had given him. What abilities has God given you?

_____

Which of these do you most enjoy using?

_____

❏ I've found a prayer partner, and we've started meeting together. (See the guidelines on pp. 32-33.)

THE F.A.W.M.* KID STRIKES AGAIN

YOU ARE REALLY F.A.W.M.

FANATIC AND WEIRD MADMAN?

FINE ACCOUNTANT WANTING MORE?

FRANKLY AFTER WIFE'S MONEY?

FULLY AWESOME WITH MEN?

* FEARFULLY AND WONDERFULLY MADE (PS. 139:14)

If you were to describe your role in your church "body" (or youth group) in terms of a part of the human body, what part would you be? Why?

_____

_____

As you look at your church or youth group, which gifts or abilities seem to be appreciated the most? On the list below, put a 1 for "very much appreciated," a 2 for "somewhat appreciated" and a 3 for "not generally appreciated."

_____ Preaching
_____ Organizing
_____ Playing piano/guitar/other instrument
_____ Teaching
_____ Singing
_____ Sports ability
_____ Leading a group
_____ Technical know-how
_____ Showing compassion
_____ Knowledge
_____ Artistic talent
_____ Encouraging others in their faith
_____ Serving
_____ Working with children
_____ Other gifts: _____

_____ _____

Do you think this is right? Are there certain people who should be appreciated more than others for their role in the "body"? If not, what could you do to help change the situation?

_____

_____

❏ I'm praying the Prayer for the Body of Christ.

TUESDAY

READ
Romans 12:3-10

Who's the most important person in your church? In your youth group? Don't even think about it, because a Bible passage like this one makes those questions dumb. We have different gifts, it says. Each one of us is important.

We're like a screen door. Which string of metal is most important? They all are! If one breaks, it leaves a hole for the insects to get through, and the whole door is useless. All the parts must do their job.

What other examples or analogies can you think of?

The church (or youth group) is like: _____

_____

_____

When Paul says, "Do not think of yourself more highly than you ought," he's talking to some of us who are too proud of our God-given gifts. But others are too shy about their gifts. Check whichever statements apply to you:

❏ I think too highly of my gifts.

❏ I have a healthy appreciation for my gifts.

❏ I ought to appreciate more highly the abilities God has given me.

❏ I should encourage others in the use of their gifts.

❏ I've made arrangements to try a new job in my church. (See Action Step 4 on pp. 10-11.)

● ● ●

• OPEN UP TO A PRAYER PARTNER •

▶ SESSION 1

Start with a fun question, to get you talking about yourselves a little. Here's an idea:

❏ Who's your favorite actor, musician or sports star, and why?

Now let's get a little more serious.

❏ When in your life have you been especially aware of God's presence?

Look at the covenant on the next page. Read it over carefully. Be sure these are promises you can keep. Discuss any hesitations you may have. When you're ready, sign the covenant.

Begin to compile a prayer list. Each of you could come up with one specific thing to thank God for and a couple of needs to pray about. These concerns might have to do with things like school, family or friends.

Pray together about these needs. And don't forget to thank God for the good things he's done. You may want to take turns praying. Or, you might want to launch short "sentence prayers" as you think of specific items.

Before you leave, set up another time to get together. And be sure to keep your prayer list for next time.

▶ SESSION 2

Start with more fun stuff.

❏ What's the funniest thing that's happened to you in the last couple of weeks?

Now consider a more serious question:

❏ What's one thing you've learned during this Adventure?

Take out your prayer list from last time and update it. Are there answers to thank God for? Are there other needs to add?

One more question. This may be tough. Talk about it as much as you feel comfortable doing.

❏ Is there an area where you're struggling spiritually? In other words, is there a certain sin that tempts you constantly? A particular step in your spiritual growth that you're stumbling on right now? How are you progressing on the Adventure?

Remember not to judge each other. We all have struggles, and you can seek God's help together.

Pray for each other about these spiritual needs and the other items on your list.

Set up another time to get together.

▶ SESSION 3

❏ What would you do with $500,000?

❏ What person has affected your spiritual life the most?

Talk about the spiritual concerns you shared last time. Have you seen progress?

What new needs have come up? How's the Adventure going for you? If you're struggling, is there a step you could take in the next week or so that might help?

Update your prayer list. Pray together about all of this, but especially for strength to take that positive step in your spiritual life.

Arrange your next meeting time.

▶ SESSION 4

❏ If you could ditch school for a day, how would you spend that time?

❏ If God gave you the power to work one miracle for someone else, what would it be?

Check up on that positive step you talked about taking in your spiritual life. How did it go? What other steps may lie ahead?

Update your prayer list. Think about your church or youth group. As you review the "dysfunctions" we've been talking about, where is your group's area of greatest need? Note the two extremes listed in the columns below.

NEEDY	DOING OKAY
Not listening	Listening to God and each other
Love based on performance	Freely loving, affirming
Blame-shame syndrome	Forgiving, helping
Unhealthy competition	Appreciating each person's gifts
Denial	Openness, honesty

Pray for this area of need. Continue to pray for your spiritual growth and the other items on your prayer list.

After this session, you're on your own. You may want to continue getting together every so often to share and pray. Talk about this, and arrange your next meeting time.

COVENANT

We're joining in a prayer partnership for the 50-Day Adventure. We agree:

_____ To meet at least four times during the Adventure.

_____ To keep secret anything we talk or pray about when we get together. We need to be able to trust each other if we're going to open up.

_____ Not to judge the problems or doubts shared by our partner. Instead, we'll be accepting of one another.

_____ Not to try to solve each other's problems during these meetings. Our purpose for getting together is to share and pray.

Signed _____

_____

_____

What was God's purpose in giving gifts?

_____

What does that say about how we should use our gifts?

_____

_____

What is one way in which you could "build up" the body of Christ?

_____

Don't miss the rich words of verse 13: "unity," "mature," "whole measure," "fullness." What place does competition have in all this?

_____

❏   I'm praying the Prayer for the Body of Christ.

A GOOD IDEA GONE WRONG

Have you met with your prayer partner yet? Remember, we encourage you to meet four times during this Adventure, and you're more than a third of the way through it already.

Today's passage gives us a glimpse of an ancient prayer partnership—David and Jonathan. You may need some background.

Saul is the king. David has already been anointed as the king-to-be. Saul doesn't like this one bit, and he's out to kill David. So David's hiding out in the desert. Jonathan is Saul's son, prince of Israel. This would give him every reason to join his father *against* David, but what does verse 17 tell us about Jonathan's outlook?

_____

_____

David also would have good reason *to mistrust* Jonathan, but instead they have forged a deep friendship. Notice that Jonathan "helped him find strength in God." What does that mean? How can you do that for your prayer partner?

_____

_____

_____

_____

❏ This week I chose someone to affirm, and I've noted what I said on p. 63.

FOCUS: Christians should be honest with one another.

CONTRASTING DYSFUNCTION: Denial and delusion—pretending problems don't exist.

POSSIBLE RESOURCES: Your pastor's sermon; The Chapel of the Air broadcasts; chapter 4 of *Healing the Dysfunctional Church Family* (see p. 14).

▶ SUGGESTED PRAYER OF PREPARATION

Lord,
I praise you for your truthfulness in dealing with people. You don't sweep problems under the rug, but you're always up-front and honest with us. You call us to be open with you as well, because you already know all our thoughts, feelings and concerns.
Amen.

FRIDAY

DAY 20

READ
Isaiah 45:18, 19

Focus on verse 19. God says he doesn't play hide-and-seek with us. He tells us what we need to know. How does God communicate with you?

_____

_____

One of the great things about God is how down-to-earth he is in his communication. Even in these two verses, he speaks directly and honestly: "Listen, guys, I'm not trying to fool you!" What could this tell you about the way you communicate with God?

_____

_____

❏   I'm continuing to meet with my prayer partner, using the guide-lines on pp. 32-33.

SAT / SUN
DAYS 21 & 22

▼

READ
Psalm 119:43-48

S **ome** may be surprised that the psalmist puts together "freedom" and God's commands (verse 45). We're used to having a pile of dos and don'ts that restrict our freedom. But there is a great truth here.

Take my computer. (Please!) When something goes wrong with my word-processing program, I often wish I could call the person who wrote the software and find out how to fix it. Fortunately, I have a manual. The one who created the software tells me in that book how the program's supposed to work. At first glance, the manual may seem like a lot of silly rules. ("Don't put your diskette in the dish-washer or microwave. Don't play frisbee with it." Stuff like that.) But the result is that the program works better. In fact, the manual even tells me about exciting new things I can do with my word processor that I never dreamed of.

So it is with the Bible. The One who created _me_ offers his man-ual to tell me how I work best. If there are glitches in my system, the Bible will help me troubleshoot. And it opens up exciting new options. As I "seek out God's precepts" I can truly "walk about in freedom."

Have you ever experienced freedom by following God's com-mands? When?

_____

_____

_____

❏   I'm praying the Prayer for the Body of Christ.

● ● ●

It was a cover-up that almost worked. David messed around with Bathsheba and had her husband killed in battle. David must have seemed like a hero when he married the grieving war widow. Maybe some insiders knew the real story, but they weren't talking. Except for the prophet Nathan.

How do you think Nathan felt as he approached the king?

_____

_____

What was Nathan's message?

_____

_____

_____

How did David respond?

_____

_____

_____

(For more insight on David's feelings, read Psalm 32:1-5.)

❑   I'm continuing to meet with my prayer partner, using the guidelines on pp. 32-33.

Why do you think Adam and Eve didn't go right to God and confess their wrongdoing?

_____

Do you ever try to hide from God? How?

_____

_____

Why do you think we human beings tend to deny our problems and run away from them?

_____

_____

❏ I've made arrangements to try a new job in my church for Action Step 4 (see pp. 10-11).

If two people showed up at your school, one of them a "new self" kind of person and the other an "old self" kind of person (verses 22-24), what would they each be like?

"New self" person: _____

_____

"Old self" person: _____

_____

Which of the following are appropriate ways to "speak truthfully" to others (verse 25)?

- ❏ Telling the person behind you in church that you wish he'd sing more softly because his voice is so bad
- ❏ Being angry at another member of your youth group but not getting even, just holding a grudge
- ❏ Telling your parents how much you appreciate them
- ❏ Letting your parents know when they tick you off
- ❏ Unloading all your problems on a caring friend

Ephesians 4:15 says we should speak the truth *in love.* Pick one of the situations you checked above. Write down what you could say to *lovingly* speak the truth in that situation.

_____

_____

Note the wording of verse 26. " 'In your anger do not sin.' Do not let the sun go down. . . ." You *will* get angry, so *deal with it.* Talk about it. Be honest (but loving). Don't let your anger fester and turn into something worse.

- ❏ I'm praying the Prayer for the Body of Christ.

● ● ●

Nice story. What does it mean?

Try this: Jesus helps us do amazing things.

Krista is worried about an English exam. "Lord, help!" she cries the night before. "All right," Christ says. "Turn off the CD player, unplug the phone, and let's get busy." She studies hard and aces the test. Do you think this can really happen? _____

Scott wants to tell his friends about Jesus, but he's too shy. He talks to the Lord about it and the next day, over lunch, a guy says, "So what do you think about this life-after-death thing, anyway?" Scott talks about Jesus and heaven. Could this sort of thing happen to you? _____

What "amazing" thing could Jesus help you do in the next month?
_____

Action Step 4 has you "playing" at a new job in your church. You may be afraid of this. That's understandable, but remember this Scripture passage. Let down your net and let Jesus do the rest.

(To review Action Step 4, see pp. 10-11.)

❏ This week I chose someone to affirm, and I've noted what I said on p. 63.

TOPIC 5

STRATEGY SESSION

FOCUS: Christians can be free from destructive life-patterns.

CONTRASTING DYSFUNCTION: Compulsive/addictive behavior, especially related to your church or youth group.

POSSIBLE RESOURCES: Your pastor's sermon; The Chapel of the Air broadcasts; chapter 5 of *Healing the Dysfunctional Church Family* (see p. 14).

▶ SUGGESTED PRAYER OF PREPARATION

Lord,

I praise you for your power to make all things new. You call us to break free from compulsive patterns that inhibit or control us, so that we can enjoy the wholeness you offer. Thank you for often surprising us by bringing healing to our lives in creative ways.

Amen.

FRIDAY

DAY 27

▼

READ
Ephesians 3:14-21

HOW many times in these verses do you find the word *power?* _____ What does Paul say about it?

_____

_____

If you lived the next 24 hours with a strong awareness that Christ was "dwelling in your heart" (verse 17), what difference would that make?

_____

Consider this: Paul wrote these verses to a church. As you look at your church or youth group, what do you think needs to be "made new"?

_____

What can you do to help?

_____

❏ I'm continuing to meet with my prayer partner, using the guidelines on pp. 32-33.

SAT⁄SUN

DAYS 28 & 29

READ
Psalm 145:1-7

Jason is sitting in church, trying to follow the sermon, but he is also very aware that the lovely Christine is sitting beside him. His thoughts also drift to the championship game being played that afternoon. And he worries a bit about a paper he has to write for school.

But the pastor is bringing new energy to the text of Psalm 145. Suddenly, from the pulpit, he says, "Jason, why don't you tell of the power of God's awesome works, as it says in verse 6?"

"Excuse me, sir?" Jason pipes up, stunned. After all, this is church, not history class.

"It says, 'I will proclaim your great deeds.' Come on, Jason, what 'great deeds' of God would you like to proclaim?"

If you were in Jason's shoes, what would you say?

_____

Don't miss verse 4. The knowledge of God is passed from one generation to another. Ideally, family members nurture each other in the love of God. But that doesn't always happen as it should. Is there one thing you would like God to "make new" in your family?

_____

Is there something you can do to help?

_____

(You may want to talk about this with your pastor or youth leader.)

❏ I'm praying the Prayer for the Body of Christ.

M⊙NDAY

Trait: Lying

Case: Abraham and descendants (Isaac, Jacob and sons)

Example A: Genesis 12:10-20
Who lied? _____
About what? _____
Who went along with it? _____
What was the result? _____
_____

Example B: Genesis 26:6-11
Who lied? _____
About what? _____
Who went along with it? _____
What was the result? _____
_____

Example C: Genesis 27:5-13
Who lied? _____
About what? _____
Who went along with it? _____
What was the result (see verse 41)? _____
_____

Example D: Genesis 37:23-35
Who lied? _____
About what? _____
Who went along with it? _____
What was the result? _____
_____

If you were counseling any of these people, what would you advise
them to do to break this family chain of deception?
_____
_____

❏   I'm continuing to meet with my prayer partner, using the guidelines on pp. 32-33.

44

According to these verses, how can you please God?

_____

Does this passage make you aware of some pattern in your life or your family that needs to be corrected?

_____

Read Ephesians 5:8-14.
According to these verses, how can you please God?

_____

Does this passage make you aware of some pattern in your life or your family that needs to be corrected?

_____

Read Ephesians 5:15-20.
According to these verses, how can you please God?

_____

Does this passage make you aware of some pattern in your life or your family that needs to be corrected?

_____

❏ I've made arrangements to try a new job in my church for Action Step 4 (see pp. 10-11).

WEDNESDAY

READ
Hebrews 5:11-14

What is the problem the author is addressing in this passage?

_____

About how long have you been a Christian?_____

If you asked God to determine your spiritual age (your maturity in the faith), which category do you think he would put you in?

❑ preschooler   ❑ grade-schooler   ❑ high school student
❑ young adult   ❑ middle-aged person   ❑ senior citizen

If you *are* just a baby in the faith—say you've become a Christian in the last year or so—there's nothing wrong with learning the basics. That's the "milk" the author is talking about.

But you won't stay there forever. Eventually, you'll grow into "meatier" teaching. You'll dig more deeply into the nature of God.

Many of the compulsions and addictions we're discussing in this Adventure have something in common: People aren't growing up. Sometimes you'll hear psychologists talk about "adult children." They're referring to people who are still fighting the battles of their childhood, trying to prove themselves, win approval, "find themselves."

As a young person, you can take your time growing up. But do allow yourself to become a *mature* child of God.

NOTE: If you're not sure what your "spiritual age" is, or what it means to "become a Christian," talk to your pastor or youth leader or another believer.

❑   I'm praying the Prayer for the Body of Christ.

● ● ●

THDAY 33URSDAY

H **ave** you been meeting with your prayer partner? To complete Action Step 5, you probably should have met at least twice by now. As you've prayed and talked together, most likely you've felt strengthened in your faith.

Look through today's passage and jot down any words or phrases that show how Christians have a good effect on one another.

_____

_____

_____

_____

_____

Here's one you might have missed. In verse 1 we see that Paul was not alone in writing this letter. He had the support of Silas and Timothy.

In verse 2, we find the authors praying for the church at Thessalonica. As you pray for your church (or youth group), what three specific things could you pray for?

❶ _____

❷ _____

❸ _____

Why not share these requests with your prayer partner?

❏ This week I chose someone to affirm, and I've noted what I said on p. 63.

T⊙PIC 6

STRATEGY SESSION

FOCUS: Christians should allow one another to make mistakes.

CONTRASTING DYSFUNCTION: Perfectionism.

POSSIBLE RESOURCES: Your pastor's sermon; The Chapel of the Air broadcasts; chapter 6 of *Healing the Dysfunctional Church Family* (see p. 14).

▶ SUGGESTED PRAYER OF PREPARATION

Lord,
I praise you for your grace. You're not surprised that we sin, and you graciously forgive us when we ask your pardon. So we don't have to struggle to hide our problems or pretend we're perfect. Your Spirit lives inside us and helps us to become more like Christ.

Amen.

FRIDAY

DAY 34

▼ READ
1 Timothy 1:12-17

DO you ever feel that God couldn't possibly like you? If so, when was the last time you felt that way?

How does Paul describe himself in today's passage?

Despite Paul's bad behavior, God "poured out" his grace on him (verse 14). Picture a pitcher of water being poured over your head on a blazing hot day. It washes away the dirt and sweat and heat.

If God poured out *words* rather than water, what words of grace might he say to you?

At first glance, this passage doesn't seem to make sense. We're sinners. And yet verse 16 says we can approach God's throne "with confidence." How can that happen?

Our first clue: What is God's throne called ? _____
This tells us how God deals with us.

Then look back at verse 15. Jesus is our High Priest. In this role he deals with God on our behalf.

The same verse says Jesus is able to "sympathize" with us. Why is that?

_____

What is the strongest temptation you've faced in the last week?

_____

Jesus faced that same temptation! He knows how tough it is! That means he can **A.** help us withstand temptation, and **B.** forgive us when we blow it.

❏   I'm continuing to meet with my prayer partner, using the guidelines on pp. 32-33.

THE DANGERS OF TYPOGRAPHICAL ERRORS

49

M⊙NDAY DAY 37

READ
Galatians 6:1-5

True–False Test

T F If a Christian sins, the church should kick him out.

T F Even "spiritual" church members may be tempted to sin.

T F We "fulfill the law of Christ" (verse 2) by making sure that no one in our church does anything wrong.

T F We "fulfill the law of Christ" by helping each other when we stumble.

T F We should be constantly comparing ourselves to others, trying to be better Christians than they are.

The key point is that Christians *will* sin. Rather than judging one another, we should help pick one another up. We ought to be striving *together* to please God, not competing.

Is there someone "caught in a sin" whom you could help? How?

_____

_____

If you're caught in a sin, who is someone you could go to for help?

_____

❏ I'm praying the Prayer for the Body of Christ.

TUESDAY

DAY 38

READ
1 John 1:8–2:2

It seems that some people in the church were claiming they were perfect. They said they had reached such a point of fellowship with God that sin didn't matter. They were beyond sin. Meanwhile, other Christians were worried. They knew they still sinned. Did that mean they were on some lower spiritual level? John wrote this letter to sort things out.

In 1:8 and 1:10, what does John say about those who claim to be sinless?

_____

_____

What happens when we face up to our sin (1:9)?

_____

_____

Does this mean we should sin whenever we want (see 2:1)?

_____

Are there sins you need to confess to God right now? Rather than writing down the details, make up code words for the sins you need to confess and write them down here.

_____   _____

_____   _____

Tell God you're sorry for these things. And be assured of his forgiveness (1 John 1:9).

❏   I've tried a new job in my church (Action Step 4), and I've completed the short evaluation form on p. 64.

Which is easier—confessing your sins to God or confessing your sins to another Christian? Why?

_____

_____

Today's passage talks about being open and praying for one another. Do you have someone you can "confess your sins" to, and pray with? _____ Would your Adventure prayer partner be someone you could do that with? _____

What good would it do to be open about your weaknesses with someone else?

_____

_____

❏ I'm praying the Prayer for the Body of Christ.

HOW NOT TO BE A PRAYER PARTNER

TH DAY 40 RSDAY

READ
2 Timothy 1:3-7

Have you tried a new ministry task for Action Step 4 yet? If not, have you made arrangements to do so? Maybe you need some encouragement. Is there someone you could talk with who might provide the encouragement you need? _____

In verse 6, Paul talks about a "gift of God" Timothy has—probably an ability to preach or teach. What does he want Timothy to do with this gift?

_____

Verse 7 implies that Timothy may have been "timid" about using his gift. What fears do you think he might have had?

_____

Do you have an idea about what *your* gift (or gifts) of God is? _____ How can you "fan it into flame"?

_____

❏ This week I chose someone to affirm, and I've noted what I said on p. 63.

A CHURCH BASED ON A BIBLICAL MISPRINT

CHURCH OF THE HESITATION
TODAYS TEXT- "GOD HAS GIVEN US A SPIRIT OF TIMIDITY"

AVERAGE ATTENDANCE? HARD TO SAY. MOST OF THEM HIDE UNDER THE PEWS.

TOPIC 7

DAYS 41–48

FOCUS: Christians should freely express their emotions.

CONTRASTING DYSFUNCTION: "Frozen" feelings.

POSSIBLE RESOURCES: Your pastor's sermon; The Chapel of the Air broadcasts; chapter 7 of *Healing the Dysfunctional Church Family* (see p. 14).

▶ SUGGESTED PRAYER OF PREPARATION

Lord,

I praise you for the depth of feelings you express. In the Scriptures we see you showing emotions that range from love and joy to disappointment and even anger. Upon Christ's triumphal entry into Jerusalem, he openly wept over her sins. To be made in your image is to have feelings. Help us learn to express our emotions appropriately so that we might reflect you more fully.

Amen.

FRIDAY

DAY 41

Jesus told a story about a kid who ran away from home. The father in the story clearly represents our heavenly Father, God. The kid stands for all of us who have strayed from God and are welcomed back home. As you read Luke 15:11-24, pay attention to the deep feelings shown by the father. These are God's emotions.

How do you think the father felt at the following points in the story?

Verses 11, 12: _worried, sad_

Verses 13-16: _____

Verses 17-20: _____

Verses 21-24: _____

Continued

54

Does recognizing these feelings make God seem more personal to you, or not? _____ How does it make you feel?

_____

❏ I'm continuing to meet with my prayer partner, using the guidelines on pp. 32-33.

SAT/SUN ▼ DAYS 42 & 43

Jesus told another story about a father and son. This time the son represents Jesus himself, sent as a messenger to the "tenants" on God's property. Read Matthew 21:33-40.
 What might have been the landowner's feelings at the following points in the story?
Verses 33, 34: _____
Verses 35, 36: _____
Verses 37-40: _____

FEELING CHECK! Sometimes it's good to stop and think about how you and those around you are feeling, including God. As you go through this weekend, stop a couple of times and ask, "How is God feeling about this right now?" *Be sure* to do this a couple of times during your church's worship service. Picture God enjoying the praise of his people.
    Record some of your findings here:

Time of "Feeling Check"	How I Think God Felt
_____	_____
_____	_____
_____	_____

❏ I'm praying the Prayer for the Body of Christ.

READ
Luke 19:28-44

A glorious scene! But it's not all happiness. How do you think Jesus felt at the following moments?

Verses 36-38: _____

Verses 39, 40: _____

Verses 41-44: _____

What did Jesus have to be happy about?

_____

_____

What did he have to be sad about?

_____

_____

What did he have to be angry about?

_____

_____

❏ I'm continuing to meet with my prayer partner, using the guidelines on pp. 32-33.

TUESDAY

DAY 45

Wait a second! Is this the "meek and mild" Jesus we all know and love? What's he doing vandalizing the temple complex? How would you describe his feelings at this moment?

_____

Why did he feel so strongly about what was going on?

_____

Does this mean it's okay for us to be angry sometimes? Even to express our anger in strong ways? _____

Of the following choices, which do you think is best, second best, and so on?

_____Pretending you're not angry

_____Suppressing your anger for the moment, but later taking it out on someone else

_____Hitting the person you're angry with

_____Speaking strongly to the person you're angry with, and explaining why you're upset

_____Examining whether your anger is justified

❏ I've tried a new job in my church (Action Step 4), and I've completed the short evaluation form on p. 64.

FROM THE WATERED-DOWN SO AS NOT TO OFFEND ANYONE VERSION (THE WDSANTOAV)...
JESUS SCOLDS THE MONEYCHANGERS

NOW, CERTAIN UNFAIR BUSINESS PRACTICES HAVE COME TO MY ATTENTION.

Jesus knew that his crucifixion was only days away. How do you think he felt about that?

_____

How do you think the following people felt in this story?

Jesus: _____

The woman: _____

Others present: _____

If this story were happening in modern times, what sort of gift might the woman bring to Jesus?

_____

What can you do this week to express your love for Jesus more lavishly?

_____

❑   I've talked to my prayer partner about whether we want to continue meeting after the Adventure.

IF WE HAD BEEN THERE . . .

LORD, THIS PERFUME COULD HAVE BEEN SOLD TO HELP OUT OUR BUILDING FUND.

THURSDAY

Set aside more than your usual reading time today. Read Luke 22:14-46 slowly, prayerfully. This is the final evening before Jesus' crucifixion. Try to feel Jesus' feelings.

How do you think he felt at the following moments:

Verses 14-16: _____

Verses 21, 22: _____

Verse 24: _____

Verses 31-34: _____

Verse 42: _____

Verses 45, 46: _____

❑   This week I chose someone to affirm, and I've noted what I said on p. 63.

● ● ●

We're still focusing on Jesus' feelings as he faced the final moments before his death. Read Matthew 27:32-50 and put your heart with his.

How do you think the following statements made Jesus feel?

"Come down from the cross, if you are the Son of God!"

_____

"He saved others, but he can't save himself!"

_____

"He trusts in God. Let God rescue him."

_____

How would you describe Christ's feelings in verse 46?

_____

_____

As you think about Christ's death, what are *your* feelings?

_____

_____

_____

How can you express them?

_____

_____

❑   I've begun a brief Adventure "report" to my pastor, youth leader or The Chapel of the Air (see the inside back cover).

TOPIC 8

DAYS 49–50

FOCUS: Christians should feel free to enjoy times of celebration.

CONTRASTING DYSFUNCTION : Not being able to have a good time.

POSSIBLE RESOURCES: Your pastor's sermon; The Chapel of the Air broadcasts; chapter 8 of *Healing the Dysfunctional Church Family* (see p. 14).

▶ SUGGESTED PRAYER OF PREPARATION

Lord,

I praise you for the way you appreciate times of celebration. You give joy to your people and rejoice with them in feasts and banquets, from the Old Testament festivals to Jesus' parties, to the Lamb's wedding reception at the end of time. This Sunday, we rejoice in Christ's great victory over sin and death.   *Amen.*

SATURDAY

DAY 49

READ
Matthew 27:57-66

F OCUS on verse 61. How do you think Mary and Mary felt as they sat across from Jesus' tomb?

_____

Have you ever felt so defeated, so despairing? When?

_____

Hold on! Aren't we supposed to be celebrating celebration? Well, yes. But what do we have to celebrate as Christians? Jesus' triumph over sin and death. If we understand how bad sin is, and what Jesus had to do to defeat it, then our joy will reach new heights when we celebrate Christ's victory.

Here's a suggestion: Let this be a "down" day for you. Take time to confess your sins before God. Think about Jesus' sacrifice. Turn off TV or other distractions and spend some time meditating on God's love. Then tomorrow we'll pull out all the stops and celebrate!

Celebrate! Jesus is risen!

How do you think the women felt when they saw the empty tomb and the angel?

How do you think they felt when they saw Jesus?

Have you ever felt this kind of joy in Christ's presence? When?

What will you do today with your family, church or youth group, to celebrate Christ's resurrection?

What could you do individually or with a friend?

Come on! Can't you think of anything better than that? Get busy! Let's have some serious festivity, okay? Can you think of a way to celebrate that's even more joyous?

That's better.

❏ I've completed a short Adventure "report" to my pastor, youth leader or The Chapel of the Air (see the inside back cover).

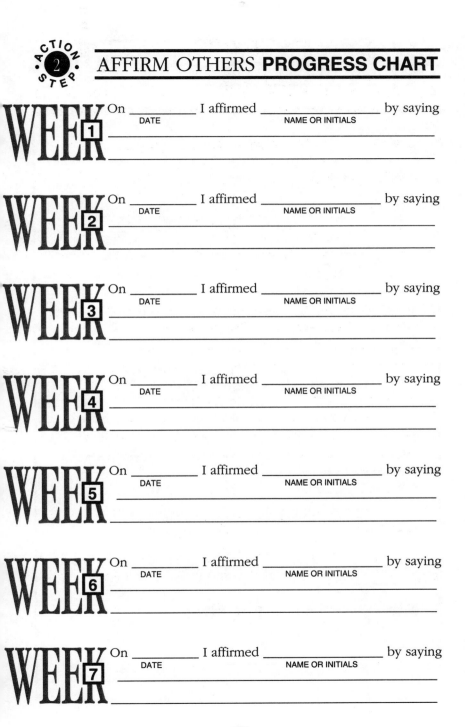

WEEK 1

On _____ I affirmed _____ by saying

DATE   NAME OR INITIALS

_____

_____

WEEK 2

On _____ I affirmed _____ by saying

DATE   NAME OR INITIALS

_____

_____

WEEK 3

On _____ I affirmed _____ by saying

DATE   NAME OR INITIALS

_____

_____

WEEK 4

On _____ I affirmed _____ by saying

DATE   NAME OR INITIALS

_____

_____

WEEK 5

On _____ I affirmed _____ by saying

DATE   NAME OR INITIALS

_____

_____

WEEK 6

On _____ I affirmed _____ by saying

DATE   NAME OR INITIALS

_____

_____

WEEK 7

On _____ I affirmed _____ by saying

DATE   NAME OR INITIALS

_____

_____

BEAT UNHEALTHY COMPETITION **EVALUATION FORM**

The task I tried: _____
_____

Brief description of what happened:_____
_____
_____
_____
_____

Is this a ministry in which I might be gifted? What feedback
have I gotten from others about my abilities in this area?
_____
_____
_____

Do I need more practice at this job to discover whether it's
something God has gifted me to do? _____

Is this task something I would like to do on a regular basis?
_____If so, how will I go about making that happen?
_____
_____
_____

Have I gained new appreciation for the people who regularly
do this job? (Name one or more of those people.)
_____
_____
_____

What is a specific way in which I might pray for them as they
perform this task regularly?
_____
_____
_____